WASP QUEEN

CLAUDIA CORTESE

Black Lawrence Press
WWW.BLACKLAWRENCE.COM

Executive Editor: Diane Goettel
Cover Art, Cover, and Interior Book Design by Martin Rock

EDITORS@BLACKLAWRENCEPRESS.COM

Published 2016 by Black Lawrence Press.
Printed in the United States.

For Grey Vild—

You made Lucy the girl she is

CONTENTS

"How deep and sticky is the darkness of childhood . . ."
—*Katherine Dunn,* Geek Love

"I haven't been this bored since I believed in Jesus."
—*Georgina Sparks,* Gossip Girl

till her arm pockmarks, that if he stops she'll expose what happens at playground's edge. Back home, Lucy decks the tree in Barbie heads, watches snow cut the landscape, all those little white knives. She leaves a hill of Jujubes where her mother's ant traps should be. Lucy loves the carmine glory of her arm, the blood medals of a champion! She calls her dog Milo to her, bites his fur till the roots let go. His yelps shine like sequins, the way snow is sequins, and her arms. Lucy demands Santa stitch her a skin of bees, that her screams be not sound but solid: a stinger that stings and stings.

LUCY LIVES IN HER GAUZE HOUSE,

a little terry cloth tumor. To live here is to be beautiful but very sad. The girls in Lucy's class tuck their hands under their thighs. They flock together like grackles. Lucy arranges pebbles in a circle, puts a G.I. Joe in the middle and lights him on fire. At night she turns the mirrors to the walls, belly to tile floor—dreams a matted mange of a pup loves her best. Lucy knows she's not like The Girls. They carry compacts in their left pockets—powder their chins, glitter their lids: a little pink goes a long way. If they opened Lucy's box, shared snickerdoodles and milkshakes, Lucy would say, I love my terry cloth house more than my mother.

WHAT LUCY'S WORLD LOOKS LIKE

Three branches strangled
in telephone wire. The chain
links of a fence.

Not the red swings behind it
but maple leaves on the slide
rotting under snow.

The oil stain on the wall
with tomato skin stuck to it.
A strip of negatives—

the photo's seared palm.
Black rings and the raccoon
crawling up the stairs.

THE FIRST MALL

was built in 1956 in a suburb of Minneapolis. Its inventor imagined a place modeled after European arcades with an aviary and hospital, post office and supermarket, where a mother sips cappuccino before a doctor pokes needles into her children's arms, a place for birds and best friends and the clean hope of brotherhood in America. Lucy spends each Friday at Mellet Mall. Mall slides are when you find an unpeopled hall and run before dropping to your knees, the combination of speed and slick floors letting you slide a long few feet. An Orange Julius is when you sip citrus cream till ice shocks your temples, peace and goodness sugaring your insides. When a boy says, "That girl has bee stings covering her face" while pointing in your direction, something formless and like blades secrets beneath skin. Frank Lloyd Wright went to the opening ceremony of the first mall in America and said, "This place is evil." When every desire feels like need, and snows tangle in each teen's eyelashes as they huddle around a joint in the parking lot's farthest corner that borders the forest, flakes turning to tears down their cheeks, it is nature's way of saying sadness will bring us together. Lucy's mother asks, "What did you do at the mall?" Ate Cinnabons and plotted the apocalypse. "Nothing much." "Who'd you hang out with?"

I called Stephanie from the payphone by the bathroom, reassuring her in my softest voice that I kill cheerleaders, bitch. "Stephanie and I had a nice chat." "Did you have fun?" A feeling like fungus spored my insides, not pain but its stupid runt sister, like when blood stickies my thighs and I realize it's not sweat but I left my Tampax at home so I fold toilet paper squares thickly and neatly in a stall and walk the halls of Taft Middle School praying that no one smells how dirty I am. "Yes."

LUCY AS LAWN STATUARY

Poured into a mold by girl hands in Vietnam then boxed to Kmart where one whitegirl kicks the elf down the aisle, her ganglion of girls cackling their mischief cackle, though the elf gets re-packaged gets sold gets her own plot of mulch and marigold. The Girls sneak out of their homes, converge in a cul-de-sac, not seeing the stone elf at garden's edge that one part of their whole had once kicked off a shelf. Camels curl from their lips—from a distance, you'd think a circus of red eyes had descended the Ohio night. Their flip-flops toe the grass, they laugh with nothing eyes, think nothing looks back—

UNCOOKED LIKE A SHEET OF TEATS,

Lucy's skin flaps from a plastic clip. The worst part isn't that she's pimply raw or sun-striped on a clothesline in a backyard. The worst part is that Lucy's a common dermis, a trite of poultry, and despite transformation from girl to dinner, a skinless chicken wanders Timberline tonight.

THE BIRDS INSIDE HER

are dying. There are blue wings at her window. Why won't you look at me, said the wren to the sparrow. The sickness starts in the trees, then pustules engulf the throat. Lucy tells her sister that ant families burrow beneath them, a small apocalypse with each step—that six-pack rings strangle sea turtles. Lucy braids grassblade and honeysuckle, crowns herself the queen of Edgemont Park. Night falls like a noose, and they leave as the molesters file in. The pomegranate is sweeter than the artichoke, and Lucy loves her sister more than her Cyndi Lauper sweatshirt.

in June heat : Lucy plucks her leg hair with tweezers :
floats her hairless body through those rotting distances
: she sees herself : knobs in her forehead : green-horned
girl limps uphill! : a darkening shriek : her dress casing
her face—

LUCY LIES

under hemlock and witch hazel, false indigo. Skin dissolves
in the fungus-dark, marrow brightens: bone-harp—wind
through rib, through clavicle, a low keening begins.

WHAT LUCY'S WORLD SMELLS LIKE

Tongue-soot, the root
chalk of rot, that egg-
y air that announces
Cleveland. Lucy wishes
for wisteria and walnut
leaf—powdered
babies lined up like calendar
days: wishes for a star, a clover,
air without seeds, oils
of orange and Ohio
June. Lucy once
walked Midland Avenue
and almost nose-orgasmed—
the honeysuckle breeze
but that's not the point here.
If I say coke's post-drip
bitters, I'll get close.
Also—high school
showers, their pubic mist,
the first spritz of Nasonex,
steroid's chemical singe—

LUCY SELFIE

A blank blue unfeeling
amid Oreos, chocolate ice cream,
last slice of pizza in the box.

LUCY LOVES THEIR DEAD EDGES,

their lying light. The dim one in the sky's eastern corner has lived a long life. A feral burst of dust, she fought and fucked her way into adulthood, settled into her bed of gold and told the circling moons of her youthful storms—their most numinous moments. Brighter than fire and cardinal, ruby Ring Pops and maraschinos, the red star beside it has no stories to tell. In other words, Lucy loves her best of all. The spruces in the distance look like a row of pointy caps on trolls' heads, and the Oreos crunching in Lucy's ears are so loud, she fears her father will hear her mouth.

LUCY STICKS A STICK

in an anthill, carries it to the other side of the yard. Ant
sisters scurry to find their wiry brothers, their mothers
with bellies like fat black beads. Lucy scrapes the sandbox,
writes tangerine and starblade and dead girls glow prettiest.
She cuts a caterpillar. Throws one green half in the grass.
Puts the other in her mouth.

says that Edna Pontellier walked into the ocean, let water
close above her because it was her only escape from the
Cult of Domesticity, Lucy sees a group of robed housewives
kill a goat, then bow to a golden, six-foot toaster oven. She
wants to walk into the ocean before 9th period gym. Her
belly fat bounces up and down when she jogs the track.
There's a tornado watch, and the clouds look like cellulite.
Lucy hides behind a spruce while the other girls run laps;
she arrives panting and unflushed to the finish line.

LUCY'S GUIDE TO SURVIVING THE FIRST DAY OF 6TH GRADE IN 1993 IN AN OHIO TOWN THAT IS 92.3% WHITE, 3.8% BLACK, AND 3.9% OTHER

Don't eat the week before. Okay, eat, but not too much. This would be an optimal meal: four Ritz crackers garnished with sliced tomatoes dabbed in salt. You can eat more, of course, if you don't mind being a fat cunt. The morning of the Big Day, rouge your cheeks, powder your forehead, then blot any excess—you want only enough makeup to dull the glow of nerves lit with terror, not enough for anyone to see you're trying. We all know The One Who Tries Too Hard doesn't have a crew circling her locker, each girl standing with one leg straight, the other bent in an affect of perfect boredom. Pretend you're more than "Something American." Braid your hair tight at the scalp, let the ends splay at your neck and shoulders—i.e., steal another's shine: your own dulls with eggy rot. That morning, slosh mealy corn-mush into your mouth, learn what every Eater of Corn Flakes across America knows: that image of golden crisps distinct in their bed of milk on the box's front is a myth. Let the milk-sog mush so much disgust into your mouth that you only eat half the bowl. Fat cunts gorge themselves on cereal the first day of sixth grade. Don't be a fat cunt. Tie your dad's leather belt around your sagging jeans and pull a Nirvana t-shirt with a yellow smiley face on the front over your soggy body. Wear a flannel, so the principal doesn't see the back. Flower Sniffin Kitty Pettin Baby Kissin Corporate Rock Whores. Let the glorious knowledge of that glorious anthem pulsing along your spine carry you through your first day. It will feel something like patriotism like pride like battle fervor—the feeling you imagine each neighborhood tree with a yellow ribbon tied to its trunk must have: something jangly and flat. When you get to school, forget you arrived busty and without a chance. The synonym for girl is dead opossum. Pretend you don't know that. Pretend you're cool, and skinny. Stand by Tiffany's locker with your hair in braids, one leg straight, the other bent. Think to yourself, "I'm all that and a bag of chips," as you twirl your braids around your finger. If she doesn't look your way, your fat-cunt-self ghosting the edges of her crew, it's okay. To be unseen is to be safe. Another name for sixth grade is Nothing Exists Outside the Mirror. Watch Channel One in homeroom as Anderson Cooper describes Yasser Arafat and Yitshak Rabin signing a peace accord. If you don't understand what that means, don't worry. You probably never will. If a salt burn redolent of fresh cum thickens in your throat, a taste more tactile than flavor, ask to use the hall pass. No teacher says no on the first day—especially to girls like you. Go to science class. Go to social studies class. Go to gym class. Don't change. If you do, Tiffany will stare as you lift your glorious Nirvana shirt. Your skin will prickle with the cartoon snickers worming from her mouth. Go to lunch. Here's how you'll win the cool kids over. Pull three Pixy Stix from your pocket. Spill them onto the table. Use a notebook page to razor the dust into perfect pink lines glittering like unicorn bones ground to glint powder. Remember your favorite song in *Rainbow Brite and the Star Stealer*, the one where the color kids croon, "Everybody's got a part to play to start each day in a beautiful way," as you snort sucrose through a striped straw. Don't scream when sugared fire flames your nostrils. Just smile and hold on to the song in your head. This will surely prove you're full of perfect boredom. The sugary fire: meh. The high after: meh. The boys and girls chanting "snort, snort, snort:" meh. When the principal witnesses your parody of 1970's porn parties and drags you to the office: meh. If a boy named Mike or Tom or Conner approaches after last period, asks you to hang out at the abandoned railroad tracks in the forest behind the school, because of course there are abandoned tracks in the forest behind the school, say no. Don't shrug and follow him. If he kisses you, you will become the story others survive. Walk home, but not too fast. Stop at the Sunoco and buy a can of 7Up so old, its emerald sheen has dulled to shit-green. Let the carbonation burn your buds. Pretend your body's turning on itself, that the hurt of lemon spritz comes from within.

One likes to slap slap bracelets during Civil War class—she enters the cafeteria
        transformed into the pink zebra of Taft Middle School.
One says, "Slip the cherry cigars in your pocket while I eye
        the aisle for the rent-a-cop eager to grab any girl."
One pockets Watermelon Bubble Yum and *Tiger Beat.*
        One slashes her hand then smacks her mother's face
with a freshcut palm—"You have AIDS now, bitch,"
     she hisses. Her dream recurs each night: a field beeps
once then again until hundreds of beeps chorus into one shriek—
        pagers pleading with the need of a hundred teens:
someone call me back, someone see the number,
        someone look someone ask someone keep me safe.
One read every *Baby-Sitters Club* book and doesn't read anymore.
        One got a third hole gunned into her lobe by Chrissie whose bangs
achieve an impossible verticality with the miracle of Aqua Net,
        and that one can't decide what's more cool—
her hole or Chrissie's arm of scrunchies. One cannot sleep. One sleeps too much.
        One sleeps better beneath trees than beside her father.

THE MOTHER ON TIMBERLINE LANE SCREAMS

when redrum corn syrups her face
in the bathroom mirror. A Heinz bottle shines from the shower rack

where her shampoo with infusions of artisanal cucumber and melon
had been. She growls, "Lucy, get out!"

—her one and only child, the cherub of her eye,
won't be babysat by this snot who bloodied

her mirror and stole the shampoo she bought
for twenty dollars from Bath and Body Works at Mellet Mall.

The mother can't sense the silence that locks Lucy's throat
is two parts shame, one part fear, can't feel how Lucy's voice

thickens to stuck when she tries to speak, and even if she could,
it wouldn't stop the mother from thinking, Bitch—

no, let's be honest, she'd think, Cunt. Lucy wants a name
for the mothers of Timberline Lane, a special word like stone fired

across three centuries with a hood stuffed down its throat,
a word that sluts the air with too many syllables, slits fat

from bone. Lucy cuts a cardboard lid from its box,
takes an azalea Crayola and a lime Crayola

and writes across the brown lid: Kiss the Bearded Clam.
She draws squares in Azalea and Lime, each one with a clam inside,

leading to the big clam at the end. She brings her game to Claudia's
house, the only babysitter in the Club who's worth a shit.

Dawn has the personality of Wonder Bread
and Mary Anne's as intriguing as a fly's wiry leg

but Claudia is electric rainbows is art is the hand
that flicks the BIC that sets the cul-de-sac on fire.

Lucy tells Claudia to roll the dice, prays she'll reach the clam.

LUCY LOOKS IN THE MIRROR AND SEES

a lidless eye. A hole of lye. The herpes sores the nun's
slideshow glowed before their sixth-grade horror. Sees
hairless cat. Trash bag a raccoon teethed open, (if I don't
eat for one whole week, she bargained, if I stitch my lips—)
its Kool-Aid pool ant-stuck and sunning.

LUCY PLAYS HER FAVORITE GAME

on repeat: Tape the news of Jessica lifted from the well.
Rewind slowly, watch her return to her hole.

ITS SUN-GREEN SHEEN OPENS

like a lidless eye, neon O promising pruned fingers, games that toy with death, sudden patches of warmth in cold water where urine has slipped through spandex. Lucy dips her head down and Stephanie dips her head down and they stare with burning eyes and scream bubbles of muffled sound. They break the surface with laughing, bobbing heads that chortle chemical water from nostrils. These are the rules: Dip down, open eyes, scream, "Fuck!, Shit!, Cunt hole!, Bitch-ass motherfucker!," etc. Stay underwater till slurs buoy your body and you split the surface, huffing for breath. Then, begin again. Warning: the consensual nature of this game may occasionally give way to rapey play—Lucy holding Stephanie's head down or Stephanie holding Lucy's head down.

Lucy climbs out of the pool first. Stephanie's brother points his finger out his bedroom window, shouts, "Yuck! Gross!" Lucy sees sunlight pooling into the divots that curdle her thighs, and her throat froths with disgust. As she scurries to her towel, red liquid strings down her leg. Unsure what prompted the brother's revulsion—the sight of a 13-year-old girl with cellulite or the sight of a 13-year-old girl with uterine lining down her leg—Lucy mumbles "see ya" to Stephanie and sprints back to her house next door.

Lucy eventually forgets that day at Stephanie's pool, though she dreams monstrous teeth feast on her bones after blood-liquid has seared off skin. She dreams poolwater lifts from its concrete bed, puckers like lips and kisses her till she's breathless and dying. She dreams a theater of boyfingers point at her spot-lit and paralyzed form.

and sticks them inside her. At night, the slick tip of a pillow grows between her thighs. She sees a planter man, thick and tall, blond bush crowning his head. Sees a chained dog bite the air to his left. When Lucy pees, marbles drop. The gas station's sign buzzes G s St tion.

WHAT LUCY'S WORLD FEELS LIKE

Lawnmower's teethy jangle—
too pretty.
Let me start again: drill

before anesthesia takes hold, nerve burn.
Nail shaved to bone, its
bloodthrob. Maw

of mother-smile, incisor
tine, the bridge
negotiating two wars,

a red dress, wire
hanger, the stage
deer-lit eye-lit gun-lit—

hand's first shatter—

LUCY WRAPS SALMON

around her fingers, plucks the pink flesh with her teeth.
She must wash each hand seven times. She must throw
the empty box of wild Alaskan salmon in a bag, wrap it
in red, blue, and yellow ribbons. She presses the Reddi-
wip nozzle till her mouth fills with sugary relief. Walking
down the sidewalk, Lucy waves hello to no one, counts
how long the light stays green. Reaching 20 seconds means
her mother dies in a plane crash. The sky, with its white
pelts, its glittering lid, is always with her. In her sleep a
man binds her wrists and tulip trees unpucker their lips
in the wind.

Dear made-for-Sunday dress—

I want my Adidas and sweatpants. Dear meadow, bless the
new tufts of hair in my armpits. Mother threatens, "You
must eat your porridge and whey, drink your black tea
curdled with milk, or I'll leave you at woods' edge where
howls rise up through the trees and all who enter return
with a tail between their legs, beak instead of a nose." At
night, my bed becomes the forest floor. Fur softens my
fingers. Dear moon's milk-eye, your rot-lid of calcium, I
smash my bowl against the door, throw hot tea in Mother's
face, so why won't she do as she threatens?

WHAT HER SISTER SEES WHEN
LOOKING AT LUCY—

lass in a flesh-dress with milk skin and milk teeth
and hair like oats boiled in eggspit,

the mouth lacking shame, the faraway glaze
that descends Lucy's eyes when her edges

turn edgeless, when feelings curdle so quickly
and so fully all else vanishes

and she becomes everything-at-once
like water boiling the steel skin from a kettle,

though the kettle's shape remains so the liquid
becomes a kettle-shaped form, fluid and searing—

what some call blind rage
doesn't mean Lucy cannot see, it means

she sees so much, sight can't contain it,
and she throws a wingback chair at her father's torso,

she cracks her sister's temple on the chaise lounge,
she tears divan cushions with her teeth,

shows—beyond the catalog promises
of comfy, ergonomic, guaranteed or money returns—

furniture's many uses.

LUCY REMEMBERS

meathooks in Arctic air, their shiny longing for de-furred forms,
       bone lipid, for fat greasing steel fingers—bodies
                    hanging that had once gnawed grass

stitched white by a fence beneath clouds so bulbous
              up-lookers forget the holes

      air conditioners across America had bit into sky.
           Lucy exits the meat factory,
toes a tuft of weeds. This field trip

is her favorite: concrete's edge: Axe cologne: mold
          blackening the bus corner, and Lucy's sudden realization—

    If Polly Pocket can say, No, I'd prefer tea over Twizzlers;
              no, I'd rather rock my thumb-sized baby
                  in my room than on the patio;
  no, I want my husband to be astronomer not artist—
                       I, too, can refuse.

WHAT THE GIRLS NAMED LUCY /
WHAT LUCY NAMED THE GIRLS

The Girls said, "Lucy Fat Face, Ugly, Stupid, Miss Lardy Lard."

Lucy's names—

"Empire Girls Glow Wartiest,"

"Fungus Furring Basement Corner—

Dad's Stash of Sticky Mags."

"Must Girls," "Jelly-Between-the-Toes Girls," "Onion Pits" and "Missing

Eyelid"—Lucy says, "You're the toe-throb

ingrown. Your factory shrills

fang the air,

your skin the skin

of drums I bang

to break—"

fucked doll. Pawn shop musk, dust fuzzing its one finger.
If Lucy throws her in the dried-out river, no water-plop
no sun-blue sheen. Dirt doll in a dirt scar. Lucy can't
braid hair with one hand. Does that make her less girl.
She smashes the rust face in the grass, says, Don't you
love that minty smell. Then tells the doll a story: The
world was created by seven robots who wired it to end by
fire. The button that ignites the blaze is hidden deep in
a mountain and one man knows how to find it. If he gets
really really mad he will press it. The world will end in
one fiery ball big as Mars' big toe, if Mars were a foot with
a really big toe.

LUCY TILTS THE MIRROR OF THE COVER- GIRL COMPACT BETWEEN HER LEGS,

spots violet folds. A part of her body doesn't exist and then it does. Lucy bets her mother cut the hole, stitched the flaps back. She bets the doctors cheered the shearing on, their hand-claps like a mouth wired open on a treeless hill as lightning nerves the teeth electric.

LUCY WANTS TO BE ALL

Velociraptor, its blood-spark wings, wants to smash the
basil plants from the neighbor's porch one by one, twist
the tabby's tail and shave its fur to terror-shapes. She
wants to light the tallest pine, call Mother to the trees.

The air
inside a
leaf fist.
Not
October's
burnt romantics
or tin aftermath
of rain,
no mist through trees,
lone maple
on hillside green—
solitude's calm
is not the air
Lucy breathes.
When you feel
mad at
world
which means
mad at
self,
there's no
sweet alone.
Midsummer sewer,

trash, rat dung
is the wind
through Lucy's hair,
meaning—
I'm ugly
stupid
my cottage cheese
thighs
and bubble ankles
in one beige sock
one white.

squares of wood and wire. Each smile, each sister in the flowers, each brushstroke thinning to the hushed tone of a girl who can't scream in a shed in clear daylight is turned over. "Did you see me do it? You can't prove it then," Lucy says when her mother asks why each painting in the living room has been flipped towards the wall.

Lucy loved her skin
lit her
you see
until we
in between
the bully
the nails
we suffer
and then
cat-lit
the distance
that '90s kitsch

its glow-in-the-dark frame
through dark alleys
we are all body
are no longer body
we suffer
the mannequin
teeth-plucked
till suffering blooms
the alleys turn
laugh-lit knife-lit
of payphone booths
our girlhoods died in

you can't recall. No, she's the night you can—part symbol, mostly flesh, the pink gel named pus in the holy stye of the Father's eye.

ORIGIN STORY

At eight years old, Lucy began carrying caterpillars on
sticks to a big rock in the garden. She sliced them—one
wriggly half dangling from her mouth, the other writhing
on the rock. She took her mother's Schick to the tub,
scraped it up her shins till water bloomed gauzy red. She
told Stephanie, her best friend, that they should rub their
bottom parts together and when Stephanie shook her head,
Lucy smacked her. Lucy acted this way because:

A) Lucy's uncle drives her to Cleveland Indians games
every Sunday, lets her eat as many bags of Pop Rocks as
she wants from the Costco mega pack in the backseat. He
plays cassettes not of Winnie the Pooh's Don't Talk to
Strangers songs but of Wilson Phillips and Nelson and
Debbie Gibson. He lets Lucy pick the cassingle and they
listen to it over and over again. "Uncle Jack is the coolest,"
Lucy says to Stephanie after their first trip to the Indians.

B) Lucy watches the scene where Stormy jumps up and down
on a cloud, makes raindrops fall as Brite tosses a rainbow
beneath the cloud to plug the rain. A chase ensues—Stormy
riding her Skydancer, Brite atop her Starlight—while Lucy
eats Kit Kats and Pizza Hut Personal Pan Pizzas and glass
after glass of Mott's Apple Juice. At school, The Girls say,
"Miss Lucy Lard, Lucy Fat Face, Tub o' Lucy Lard."

C) Lucy reaches her arms up for a hug, and her mother pats her on the head. Lucy tells her father that she made it to the final round of the school-wide spelling bee, and he mumbles something she can't hear. When she asks her mother for more apple juice, her mother hands her a glass of milk. When she asks her father to play Legos with her on the living room rug, he nods and leaves the room.

D) Lucy feels a worm sour her belly, its wiry acids churn to her throat. The burn cools when she smacks Milo in the head. It cools when she tells Stephanie the story of two bunnies that the starving family ate without skinning or frying, their mouths furred in red pulp. It cools when she moves Miss Johnstone's chair, the class erupting in glee when she falls. The worm wasn't placed there; it arrived with her on the day of her dry birth. The story goes: her mother's water never broke. Watching *Wheel of Fortune*, a bowl of popcorn on her lap, she suddenly felt her vagina widen. She went to the bathroom, held a hand mirror between her legs, and saw the crown of a Lucy head.

E) All of the above

F) None of the above.

in flames. If she's bit one boy, she's killed none. Subtract two apples and she gets the bunch. Once was hillside. Bone cross and lake coat. Once was everything nice. Lucy ate the cherry heart the black O at television's center. Why alone in pine-shadow. Why forest. Why not cauldrons. If Lucy read the wind right. It said hubris. A theater she died in.

in the manure, prays for fire. She sits beneath the porchlight, sets her stolen vodka on the step, drinks till she burns. She spots a barn door in the frozen ground, sees blood drops on snow—girl nails, Lucy whispers and runs to the house where she stirs mint leaves in a pot of hot water, listens to the sink's silverdrip—its bright promise: that what she hears is not human.

LUCY SELFIE

Snowdrop eyelid,
hole I cannot fill.

the long hallway. Sister canters
and Lucy pours milk in her ears.
Lucy gallops by sister's door
and she freezes like a pond
begging to be broken.
They never speak of that saddle
of finest leather, how Lucy escaped
the king without her, then let his black
horses darken between them.

BLUE GLINT IN THE WOODSHED'S SKIN

follows the mother-body across yard
as it puts a ball in bin, lawn chair

in its lawn place, picking and sorting
as mother-bodies do on their mother-days

off. Zoom in and the blue has a lid, the blue
one piece of a body in a shed

chinking the woodshed's bark
with her new Swiss, making holes

where she thinks the holes should have been,
and if you peel Lucy's skin, you won't find

Christmas white, democracy of ice
jangling equally over everything:

you'll see her terror, almost sexual,
almost the cherry-hot center: cute's

opposite or rather its essence, her hole
here and there and there—

She hates herself because _____ (proper noun). Each time Lucy looks in the _____ (not mirror: what else reflects), she thinks _____, _____, _____ (expletives). She remembers watching _____ (suburban nature image: Note, the pastoral. Note, white flight. Note, mother stands in lamp-glow she sees her at the window. Note, dog blood darkens) and feeling _____ (sentimental noun) and _____ (violent noun because sincerity terrifies). She combed _____'s (girl name) hair, she washed _____'s (girl name) power-pink jeans; they _____ (sexual verb) and _____ (verb of your choosing): don't tell. She tears hair-roots, sticks marbles where she pees because _____ (i.e., basement water). The why again: _____ (what she can't forget). She chews her scab, lets go the handlebars, BB guns a bunny, kicks the fat boy, writes "Bobby sucks big dicks" on his desk, crowbars a pet turtle from its shell, safety pins her thumb-skin because _____ (you know the answer).

LUCY FEELS THE CROTCH

of the poplar as pornography, the feeling like oil sludged
to feathers so thickly no Dawn detergent can suds her
clean. Lucy dreams her mother's wrists are pinned to a
table. If she names the dream Memory would you believe
her. Once the air sizzled with chlorine and fried chicken
fingers. It was adult swim so no one heard their knees
clicking as they kissed no one saw what summered inside
them. If we recognize our happiest moment the instant it
happens it will cease to be the happiest. Lucy said yes and
Stephanie heard lettuce. The metaphor of falling in love
as if from a diving board. Lucy slips from skin to skin but
some part will always be beside that O of chemical water.

the broken fridge, then syrupy pain and Lucy spoons dirt, buries her mother's crockpot. If Lucy masturbates while reading, she knows it's a good book. Like a cat's tongue licks the inside of an elbow, skin soft with vein, words have texture and shape, desire loosed among the neighborhood opossums and lawn elves.

LUCY DOLLED

her eyes. To be pretty was to be good. Her roller skate
ambitions—the hokey pokey and pink laces, full glory of
couple skate. She wanted her pores to open like mouths,
to be *The Craft's* one-girl coven. Lucy loved any bridge over
water, any wreath marking the highway median.

can't see her can't save her. It's not Lucy's fault all girls become drifts milky gaze turned inward. The pills her father gives her are a promise a forgiveness—they have small white wings they are tender and she loves them. Lucy loathes the sky its slinked red tail but when clouds bulge with rain pills lift Lucy into their bulbous arms.

LUCY TELLS HER SISTER

that earth's core isn't fire, it's babies
burning.

begins in lime, mist that mints and tangs to sherbet, ends
in the dark crystal. If a pale unfeeling could murder, she'd
kill the guitar and easy breezy pink would waft from her
fingertips. The red bloat the tantrum emits, blue cool that
follows. Lucy was glad and then the monster. The day in
metal turns green: iPod then tree where all the sads end.

LUCY KNOWS WORDS

live in the trees, rain like locusts when she walks through
the forest. Leaves unhook the hurt that curdles in her
throat, burns behind her lungs. A cricket's wings cry all
night, its wiry torso greening her dreams. Lucy dreams
the water that splashed on her leg when she flushed the
gas station toilet gave her herpes. She dreams elephant's
liquid eyes, an ivory hospital bed—the sun a yellow sail
lifting her from her body.

jewelweed, dung, latex fruit syndrome, hymens, Spanish influenza, humans, pantsuits, stethoscopes, diphtheria, vaccines, humans without homes, cytokine storms, Axe cologne, bloodleaf, handshakes, milkshakes, a food-crusted spoon, herpes simplex 2, heirloom quilts, heirloom tomatoes, heirloom humans their wrinkled eyes, washrags, washing machines, pine trees, molars, ultraviolet spots, gas stoves, humans in yard, humans with water hoses, humans that cough, human eyeballs, pocket watches, carbon dioxide, a day without a pocket watch.

SAFE

"Not likely to be hurt, lost, or taken away."
Also, "a secure, lockable box."

and sits on the windowsill. If she reads all day and all night no one can hurt her there her window a clear hard pond begging to be unbroken. Milo bites her sister's wrist doctors stitch the clipped vein but Mother decides to keep him. Lucy keeps silver sailor buttons beside her ribbon pets their edges.

THE MILK BELLS INSIDE HER

Lucy finds a musty box of objects in her basement—plastic unicorn with a once-pink mane, Christmas ornaments, sister's St. Joan of Arc cheerleading skirt, a headband with two horns curving from each side. Lucy slips on the band and feels the worm in her belly unsour slightly, that coil of terror and anger loosen; she feels less girl, more bumpy.

At dinner that evening she wears her new head and her mother's glare burrows into her horns, though her father's stare never settles there. They chew their creamed spinach in silence. As her mother clears the plates, she grabs Lucy's horns and says, "These are ridiculous."

That night, Lucy tiptoes into the kitchen and pulls the horns from the drawer where her mother had stowed them. She puts them back on, curls into bed, and sleeps a dreamless sleep as if a bell of milk were cooling her insides. In the morning, her mother comes in the room and scoffs. At school, The Girls knock the horns from Lucy's head, call her names that could only be thought original by 12-year-olds who subsist on a diet of Twizzlers and *Saved by the Bell* reruns.

Lucy's mother removes the horns at dinner again, slips them in the drawer. Again, Lucy's father doesn't seem to notice as he chews the leftover spinach with the new side of grilled chicken. Again, Lucy wakes before her mother. She pulls scissors and Krazy Glue from the drawer, cuts the knobs off the band, drips glue across her forehead and muscles the horns onto her head. When she slips back to sleep, milk bells her insides.

After the screams and slap, the "What were you thinking? You disgust me!" her mother drives Lucy to the doctor who gives her anesthesia and shears the horns off. Lucy wakes on the exam table wearing two gauze squares. A guttural growl aches from deep behind her throat but stops almost as soon as it begins: the bell is still cooling her belly, the worm continues to unsour—that coil of anger and terror she thought would always be there has dissolved to a few flecks.

She knows she must not remove the bandages until it's too late. She brushes her teeth with the bandages on, walks to school with the bandages on, jogs the track in gym class with the bandages on, watches *Buffy the Vampire Slayer* at 8:00 on Tuesday with the bandages on.

To say the horns carry to the surface the scumgirl monster
Lucy feels herself to be is too easy because of course Lucy
feels unlovable the most unlucky girl more skincrawl ugly
than a pimply-raw chicken hung from a clothesline to
flap in the cool suburban wind. All I can say is that once
the scars hardened to two nubs beneath the gauze—once
Lucy had her forever horns—a calm bell of milk chimed
throughout Lucy's body.

LUCY LEAFS THE GRANDILOQUENT DICTIONARY

Adelphepothia: Like all goodgirls
Lucy wants her sister's bow dress
and more than that wants tresses
that knot fingers to dip
and slip inside of her sister.

Ablutophobia: Bathtub fear
because a girl-body is still a body.
Despite doll shimmer and toy soldier
Lucy won't set toe in that water.

Bawcock: One wrinkle on Shortcake's pink shoe
where skirt folded over her knee but who would hear
that small pop.

Bibliomancy: Air of Bibles its machine bees
foretell the future in their buzz-teeth.

Burke: You shop for slap bracelets
and stress balls at the mall, stop by Claire's
Boutique where a teen with permed
bangs sprayed to the ceiling guns
sapphires into your lobes

but nothing's as fun
as shopping for your own once-boy
at Burke's store for cadavers.

Kamalayka: Blood-tail darkening
the from-fridge-to-playroom trail.

of lemon curd when sugar-dazzle dwindles to bloat. More coagulant than blondly, no pure gold baby that melts to a shriek. Remember the first time words were fire-darts and wasping, that punch-gut spell. Lucy's more corduroy than shine, ragtime slump sans the ole timey fiddle. I dangle her from two sticks above a small stage, scissor her crotch till it blooms worm-sparkles.

LUCY WANTS TO BE SEXLESS

as a field. The chocolate cherries, the Cheetos and cheese Danish are delicious but not as delicious as the self-hate that follows. Lucy looks on the sunny side. She's fat but not so fat no one will love her. She fits into plane seats, her hair smells like strawberry. Still, Lucy wishes she were good which means to be without need.

A DRIED-OUT RIVER VEINS THE WOODS BEHIND

Lucy's house. Inside are Malibu Barbies, a rust-fucked train, the gold toes of tub curling into mold. She crawls among the wreckage once hidden under water's sun-blue sheen.

IF WIND COULD MAKE HOLES

in Lucy's skin, she would know
                             it loved her. If icicles

        running like glass teeth
                along the lip of the longest branch

could speak, they would say,
                To see means that you are in some way cut,

                that you are opened up—

SONNET TO LUCY

Your face, vein-lit, bone-lit, lit by fear
you are ugly, no one likes you. Smile,
Lucy, shine like a gun, and one day you'll foam
to amber and golden, a frothy
liquid all the fathers love, their sons
waiting for the day they can drink
in a spray of sprinklers, summer glassdrops,
carbamate grass, Ikea chair, an empty
their boys can't see. Lucy, the unlovely,
the tub that is lard, it seems each decade
there's a new victim, same ganglion
of girls that peck and cackle. In my vision,
you and I banshee the branches, shatter to claw
and turn one gold girl to a blubber of caw.

LUCY KNEW WHEN SHE SAW HIS GREEN EYES

sequin the brambles, heard his paws crunch into snow, he wasn't like the other boys. At night she licks his prints, glitters each hole. Bedtime Bear was once her favorite but he's lost his head, body slumped in the corner. Soon she'll find her Green Eyes, chop his neck, sew his head to Bedtime's—create her new best friend.

cured and symptoms remain, blood-run legs which means a breach occurred, how emptied of Aqua Net the hair slips so quick down the drain. One summer, Lucy made a Marlboro mansion, drew a circle with found sticks, blessed herself the Saint of Ohio. A moment can skip three generations, appear in a dream as toy ponies broken loose, appear as the welt after—more pain than the instant the mother struck her.

LUCY AS THE LAST IMAGE IN A SALVATION ARMY SCRAPBOOK

The night is light-webbed, silver-ribbed—all spearmint-scented ghost fuzz, a firefly burst of horseshit and pearls. The Kingdom of What Is Not—a blank black page. One drawing is simple motes dusting the sun-window, another is a plate of rust and moth wings. Three familiars feline the grass beneath dusk's red teeth. Two cows munch a pasture of whey and curdled egg, and one old witch sticks a needle through each eye, a hole in her skull to let the daemon out. In the final square, spider eggs hatch from Lucy's mouth.

frog tail plays bandit plays blacken one toe leave the other pinking. She plays find a place safe and unbreathing, only the eye moves. Plays razor plays marbles tossed in creek, names one water-ring Tampon, the other Blood Wart. Lucy plays with friends. Did you think I'd say alone and with weapon, the kind kids fashion—sewing needle taped to safety pin glued to tooth pick pricking Milo tail or sister lobe. What was your favorite place. Where did your shame begin. Perhaps Lucy's the beloved blonde, handlebar glitter, a party's favorite streamer. Curly-cute and her rot imagined which means alive without odor.

LUCY WANTS RED HAIR,

tits spry as sprites, to be a Siren on the riverbank,
bewitching boys with her liquid song. She'd scissor around
them, take what's hers. Lucy feeds worms to her sister,
tells her about the dying sea turtles. To love is to suffer
and to suffer is to give yourself to this world. The sun-
freckled oak will blacken, night rotting its branches, and
this Lucy vows—no boy will divide them.

LUCY'S WORLD POPPED OPEN,

a bright umbrella
of playdates and bikerides and

I'll trampoline you if you swingset me,
Lucy promised her sister

when they swished through summer,
left one girlhood and entered another—

red lip-prints on mirrors, became
girl heroes, wasp queens.

They dreamt themselves clean, rose
to their cool thrones.

LUCY WRITES HER SISTER A LETTER

There's a razor in the peach and I planted teeth beneath your bed. Stitch those stories to your eyes because only time will tell who's the wolf at your window—if his strings of saliva will bless or burn you. When I said I hoped father wouldn't hear my mouth, I meant skin remembers porch lights and barns. I know I'm the boils on your arm, the girl with horns, a pelt of bees, the stinger that stings—what blooms from the blade, self-hate and girl-hate and grown-hate. I'll never forget when we fingered the dirt and saw that it glowed. That scene in *Dirty Dancing* where Swayze holds Jennifer Grey in the water, her body breaking in lakeskin—I know it's your favorite.

Your choosing or not choosing letter A may depend on your preference for aesthetics or statistics. In the name of the poem, I hate A—its cassettes and car, the typical uncle and his typical girl, how the Pop Rocks crackled Lucy's tongue purple, how so many hard penises zipped behind so many khaki polo pants ironed straight and without stains overfill our poems—the violences both candied and familial. In the name of what I know, I honor A. Over lattes at Starbucks, one friend told me about her uncle; during a slumber party, another friend told me about her uncle; over Blue Moons at Tierney's Pub, another friend told me about his uncle.

Your choosing or not choosing letter B may depend on your story. Was *Rainbow Brite and the Star Stealer* your favorite film. Did you forget your shorts for gym class each day, sit on the floor humming as the others tossed balls into nets. Did you feel fat, monstrous, so you refused to take off your clothes. The phrase "you feel" may make this answer the most common as I ask how you felt not what you actually were.

Your choosing or not choosing letter C may depend on how inescapably white you are.

Your choosing or not choosing letter D may depend on your theories on the origins of pathology.

Your choosing or not choosing letter E may depend on how you see the circle of action and consequence. Did she disappear into food and cartoons because she no longer wanted a body. Did she cultivate flesh rolls and soggy breasts to make herself untouchable. Did her parents not look at her because they couldn't face what had happened to her.

Your choosing or not choosing letter F may depend on the fictions that you love. Do you prefer your imagination or mine. Do you want a girl for your private hurt—her actions your own. Is Lucy your daughter. Is she you.

ACKNOWLEDGEMENTS

The Baltimore Review, Summer 2012, "The field curdles" (third place winner in *The Baltimore Review's* literature contest)

Banango Street, Spring 2015, "What Lucy's World Looks Like"

Blackbird, Spring 2013, "Lucy wraps salmon," "Lucy wants red hair," (under the title "Dear Claudia") and "Lucy writes her sister a letter " (under the title "Lucy")

Cross Poetry, May 2015, "What The Girls Named Lucy / What Lucy Named The Girls"

Day One, September 2015, "Blue glint in the woodshed's skin"

DIAGRAM, April 2012, "The birds inside her" and "When Miss Johnstone"

Front Porch Journal, May 2012, "Lucy writes a letter" (under the title "Dear dirt stain & rain-freckled Snow")

Kenyon Review Online, Spring 2013, parts of "Lucy as the last image in a Salvation Army scrapbook with drawings glued to each sheet—" (under the title "Hurricane Irene Fingers My Hair")

Meridian, Spring 2012, "Lucy lives in her gauze house" (under the title "Lucy lives in a box")

Nashville Review, April 2012, "Lucy lies" (under the title "Epithalamium")

Rattle, Winter 2011, "Lucy sticks a stick" (under the title "Sarah's mother makes her long dresses of lace")

The Offing, April 2016, "The first mall," "The Milk Bells Inside Her," "Origin Story," "Answer Key for Origin Story"

Pangyrus, Spring 2015, "the dark quivers   in that corporate way" and "What Lucy Feels Like"

Phoebe, Fall 2014, "What Lucy's World Feels Like"

Rhino Poetry, Spring 2013, "Lucy tells the boy to suck" (Editor's Prize, third place)

Revolution House, Winter 2013, "Lucy knows words" and "Lucy loves their dead edges"

Stirring, July 2016, "Lucy remembers" and "What Lucy's sister sees"

Winter Tangerine Review, Shedding Skins Feature, April 2015, "Lucy looks in the mirror and sees," "Lucy Mad Lib," "Lucy loves her rust-" and "Lucy plays her favorite game"

Winter Tangerine Review, Issue 5, "Lucy plays," "Sonnet to Lucy" and "What Lucy's World Smells Like"

Some poems from this manuscript appear in the chapbook *Blood Medals* (Thrush Poetry Press, 2015)

NOTES

In "Lucy's the last lick," the phrase *"pure gold baby that melts to a shriek"* is from Sylvia Plath's "Lady Lazarus," which appears in *Ariel* (HarperCollins Publishers, 2004)

In "If wind could make holes," the final two lines are taken from Jenny Boully's *The Book of Beginnings and Endings* (Sarabande Books, 2007): "To begin means we are in some way cut, that is, we are in some way opened up."

In "The Milk Bells Inside Her," the recurring phrase "milk bell" alludes to a line from Cynthia Cruz's poem "January," which appears in *Ruin* (Alice James Books, 2006):

> Anesthesia of medicine and me,
> Beneath its warm bell of milk. My girlhood was
> Microscopic

In "Lucy's Guide to Surviving the First Day of 6th Grade in 1993 in an Ohio Town that Is 92.3% White, 3.8% Black, and 3.9% Other," the phrase "you arrived busty and without a chance" is from Lightsey Darst's poem "[A few things I learned about sex]," which appears in *Find the Girl* (Coffee House Press, 2010): "Some girls had come in busty and without a chance."

Thank you to my mother who encouraged me to become a poet and who is the kindest human I know; my father who bought me *Baby-Sitters Club* books as a girl and Tolstoy novels as an adult: you showed me how to love literature; my twin sister Natalie who is the queen of my heart—Nat, you would smash a bottle over any man's head for me, and that is love; my older brother Joe who played me Bikini Kill CDs and showed me John Waters films: you taught me weird is not wrong; Slava Balakhovskaya and Filipp Tsessarsky—my East Coast mama and papa.

Thank you to my partner, Boris Tsessarsky, for encouraging me to believe in my work. You inspire me daily with your stories and smarts, your love and laughter.

Thank you to my publisher, Diane Goettel, for giving Lucy her forever home.

Thank you to Martin Rock for designing my dream book.

Thank you to these thoughtful and generous readers: Traci Brimhall (our epic phone calls sustain me); Gillian Cummings (Fernande and Lucy are press sisters!); Jen DeGregorio (thank you for your close reading of the MS); Suzanne Holt (my first poetry mentor!); Joy Ladin (you taught me so much about writing and life); Liz Martin (copy-edit goddess!); Rusty Morrison (you saw to the core of my work—your clarity is a gift); Meghan Privitello (fellow Queen of NJ!); Grey Vild (you were right about Lucy, brilliant friend).

Thank you to my friends: Arielle Baer, Duke (Clarkson Fisher III), Serenity Fisher, Alan Hill, Uchechi Kalu Jacobson, Caleb Kaiser, Sarah Kandiko, Autumn Linn, Alex Noussias, Darin Patterson, Jessica Rohrbach, Brynn Saito, Bekah Sankey, Staci Schoenfeld, Amy Seidenverg, Mike Soto, Kem Joy Ukwu, Cori Winrock, Melanie Wilson. To anyone I am forgetting—my apologies!

Special thank you to my adolescent besties—we survived the suburbs of Ohio together: Christine Affolter, Cathy Burns, Daniel Klein, Freedom Fenton, Bethany Fleischer, Ryan Hill, Erin Kirven, Shauna Leonard, Nikki Leper, Beth and Sarah Mishler, James Motz, Brandy and Crystal Nupp, Jessica Sands, Angel Spillane, Tiffany Smith, and Andrea Thompson.

Thank you to my writing teachers throughout the years: Kat Blackbird, Tina Chang, Suzanne Gardinier, David Hassler, Kathleen Hill, Marie Howe, Kate Knapp Johnson, and Maj Ragain.

In memory of Jamie Brocker and Jon Fox, who didn't survive in body but live on inside us.

CLAUDIA CORTESE is a poet, essayist, and fiction writer. Her work has appeared in *Blackbird, Black Warrior Review, Crazyhorse, Gulf Coast Online,* and *The Offing,* among others. The daughter of Neapolitan immigrants, Cortese grew up in Ohio and lives in New Jersey. She also lives at claudia-cortese.com. *WASP QUEEN* is her first book.